Home Economics: Budgeting & Expense Tracking Worksheet

$ £ ¥ ريال ₪ €

Dr. Arthur H. Kebo

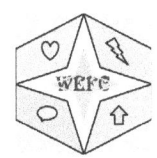

Home Economics: Budgeting & Expense Tracking Worksheet

ISBN-13: 978-1475287530
ISBN-10: 1475287534

Book Website:

> https://www.createspace.com/3865989

WordPress Blog Website:

> http://twelvefoundations.wordpress.com/

Twitter Website:

> https://twitter.com/#!/twelvefoundatio

Facebook Website:

> http://www.facebook.com/arthurkebo

Printed in the United States of America

Table of Contents

Preface

In economic hard times, everyone feels the crunch on their wallets. It seems that living costs and fuel prices are skyrocketing, while salaries and wages still remain the same. This workbook is designed to help people manage their finances and cut costs. It serves as a tool to properly plan your day-to-day and week-to-week expenses. The other book by the same author, *Save Money Checklist Worksheet Volume 1 & 2* is the second part of this financial management scheme to provide imaginative ideas to stop unnecessary waste, and save money in areas where we are often unaware of, and includes worksheets and calculation sheets to manage and track your savings strategy.

In order to manage your finances, this book provides worksheets to both calculate your budget and to track expenses. The first step in managing your weekly/monthly expenses, and to hopefully save money is to plan properly and accurately. Without a detailed, organized record, the management of finances becomes obscure and is prone to overspending. This workbook is not only for those individual who want to avoid bounced checks, falling behind on mortgage payments, and wasting hundreds of dollars every month; but, it is also for those who would like to save money for other plans, such as vacations, weddings, and extra pocket money every month.

A worksheet needs to be easy to use, and light enough to carry around. It also needs to be easily accessible, and provide extra space for notes and memos. This workbook provides lots of space to write on, and is developed to give you a ready-made budget and expense tracking tool at minimal cost. One does not need an expensive tool, unless that individual owns a business; and if it is just for personal expense management, a simple tool is always best.

At the beginning of the workbook is a detailed calculation worksheet to determine one's budget, and at the end of the workbook is a calculation worksheet to figure out the balance between the budget and weekly/monthly expense totals. This will give you an idea whether you are achieving your budget, or you need to go back and identify in the records where you are overspending, and come up with a possible way to cut cost in that area.

Everyone can do with a little extra pocket money every week. Rather than wasting money unnecessarily, it is time that you roll up your sleeves and do something to prevent money going down the drain. Only you can take that initiative by spending just a few seconds to track your expenses every day. Good luck on your path to saving money, and earning money without working for it!

Weekly / Monthly Income Calculation Worksheet

Enter your projected weekly/monthly income below:

INCOME DESCRIPTION	AMOUNT
Expected Wages / Salaries / Tips Income	+ $
Expected Pensions / Annuities Income	+ $
Expected Interests Income	+ $
Expected Dividends Income	+ $
Expected Capital Gains Income	+ $
Expected Businesses Income	+ $
Expected Credits / Refunds Income	+ $
Expected Alimonies Income	+ $
Expected Real Estate Rentals Income	+ $
Expected Other Income	+ $
INCOME TOTAL	= $

(Note: It is important that you forecast your income accurately, or else, your expenses may end up higher than your budget.)

Subtract the amount you would like to set aside for emergency (rainy day) savings every week/month:	− $

ADJUSTED INCOME TOTAL	= $

Enter this amount on the Budget Cut Conversion Worksheet on page 11.

Last Week's / Month's Expenditure Worksheet

Enter your last week's/month's total income below:

INCOME TOTAL LAST WEEK/MONTH	= $

Enter your expenses from last week's/month's expenditure record worksheets for each expense category below:

EXPENSE CATEGORY	AMOUNT	PERCENTAGE OF THE TOTAL
Food	$	%
Transportation	$	%
Entertainment	$	%
Clothing	$	%
Utilities	$	%
Shopping	$	%
Miscellaneous	$	%
Unexpected	$	%
Your Own Category #1 _____	$	%
Your Own Category #2 _____	$	%

Add the amounts above, and enter the total below:

EXPENSE TOTAL FOR LAST WEEK/MONTH	= $

Subtract the Expense Total from the Income Total, and enter the amount below. (This is the amount you overspent last week/month.):

OVER EXPENDITURE TOTAL	= $

Multiply the Over Expenditure Total by 100. Then, divide that result by the Expense Total, in order to find out the percentage you overspent last week/month, and find out approximately how much you are over budget every week/month.

(Over Expenditure Total x 100) ÷ Expense Total = Percentage Overspent

or

Over Expenditure Total		*Percentage Overspent*
————————————	=	————————————
Expense Total		*100%*

Enter your results below:

$ _____   =   _____ %

$ _____   100%

Graph the expenses for last week/month on the Weekly/Monthly Expense Record Analysis Graph on the next page, in order to give you a visual overview of your overall expense areas.

Weekly / Monthly Expense Record Analysis Graph

On the graph below, plot your last week's/month's expenses record by category percentage from page 7 with a blue or black ink pen, and analyze what your greatest expense areas are and where you overspent. Then, decide where and how much you will cut your expenses this week/month by percentage, and enter the corrected percentage with a red ink pen.

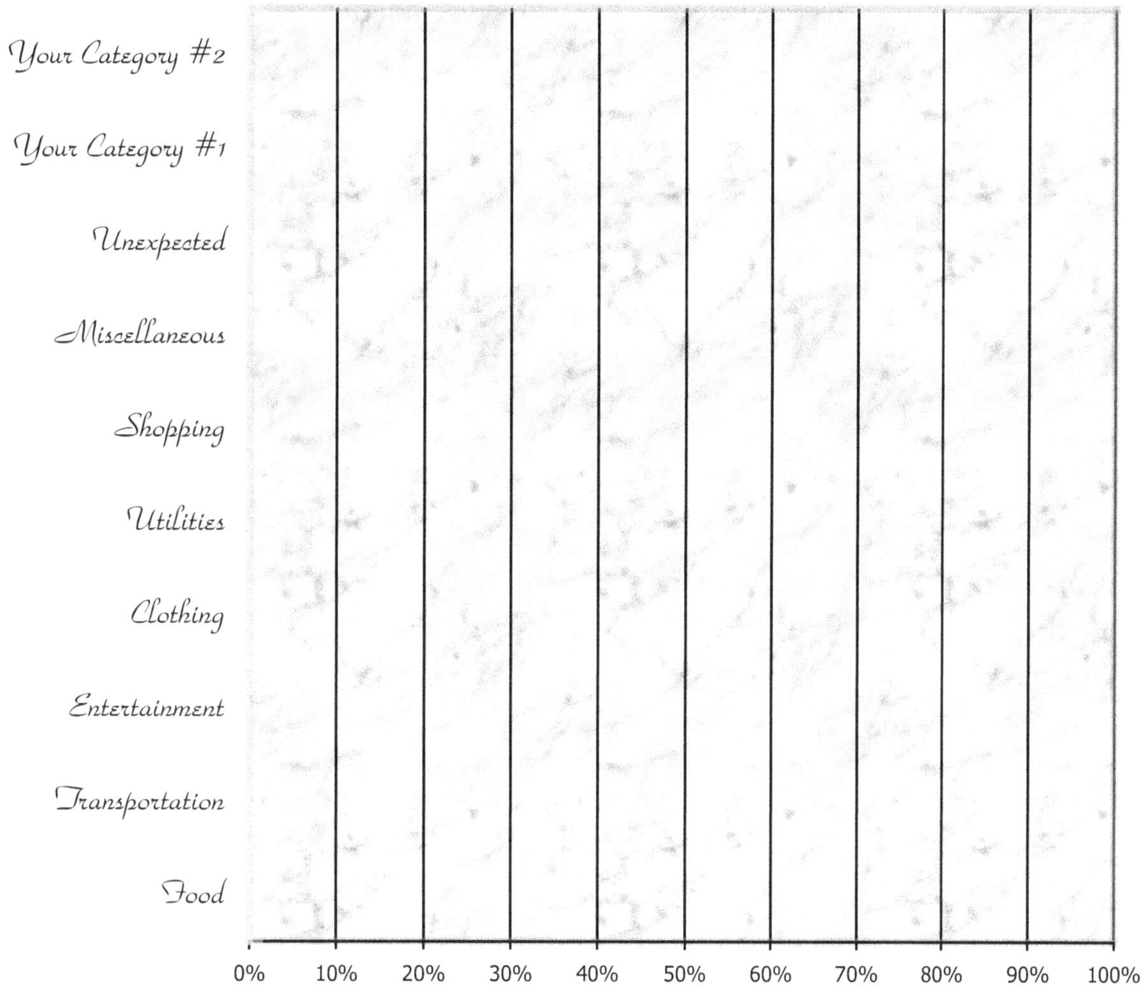

	0%	10%	20%	30%	40%	50%	60%	70%	80%	90%	100%
Your Category #2											
Your Category #1											
Unexpected											
Miscellaneous											
Shopping											
Utilities											
Clothing											
Entertainment											
Transportation											
Food											

Convert those percentage differences into dollar amounts on page 11, later.

Projected Expense Calculation Worksheet

Enter the Expense Total For Last Week/Month from page 7 below:

EXPENSE TOTAL FOR LAST WEEK/MONTH	= $

Plan your Preliminary Budget for next week/month (before calculating in the budget cuts), in each of the expense categories below, based on the information from last week's/month's expenses and your best projections for next week's/month's expenses.

(*Important: If you plan to have large additional expenses in any of the expense categories next week/month, such as hospital costs or car purchases or wedding costs, make sure you count them into your Next Week/Month Projected Expense amount.*)

EXPENSE CATEGORY	LAST WEEK/MONTH ACTUAL EXPENSE	NEXT WEEK/MONTH PROJECTED EXPENSE
Food	$	$
Transportation	$	$
Entertainment	$	$
Clothing	$	$
Utilities	$	$
Shopping	$	$
Miscellaneous	$	$
Unexpected	$	$
Your Own Category #1	$	$
Your Own Category #2	$	$

Add the amounts on the right column, and enter the total below:

PROJECTED EXPENSE TOTAL	= $

Budget Cut Conversion Worksheet

Enter the Adjusted Income Total from page 6 below:

ADJUSTED INCOME TOTAL	+$

Enter the Projected Expense Total from the previous page below, and subtract this amount from the Adjusted Income Total above:

PROJECTED EXPENSE TOTAL	−$

Enter the difference below:

BALANCE TOTAL	= $

If the Balance Total amount is a positive number, you are within budget. If the amount is a negative number, you are over budget. Calculate on the following page where and how much you will cut from next week's/month's budget.

As a first step in solving your overspending, using the budget cut information you determined on your graph on page 9, convert the expense percentage you plan to cut back from last week's/month's expenditure for each expense category into actual dollar amounts to cut from next week's/month's expenses, based on the Projected Expenses on page 10:

EXPENSE CATEGORY	PROJECTED EXPENSES	PERCENTAGE TO CUT		AMOUNT TO CUT
Food	$	%	⟶	$
Transportation	$	%	⟶	$
Entertainment	$	%	⟶	$
Clothing	$	%	⟶	$
Utilities	$	%	⟶	$
Shopping	$	%	⟶	$
Miscellaneous	$	%	⟶	$
Unexpected	$	%	⟶	$
Your Own Category #1	$	%	⟶	$
Your Own Category #2	$	%	⟶	$

Add the subtotals on the right column, and enter the Budget Cut Total below:

BUDGET CUT TOTAL	$

Subtract the Budget Cut Total from the Projected Expense Total on the previous page, and enter the amount below:

FINAL BUDGET TOTAL	$

If the Final Budget Total is less than the Adjusted Income Total, you are within budget. If the Final Budget Total is greater than the Adjusted Income Total, you are still over budget, and need to determine where else you will cut budget next week/month. If you are planning on saving money, you also need to go back and see where else you can cut your budget, in order to achieve your savings amount goal. After you have met your budget requirements or determined how to achieve your savings goal, complete the worksheet on the next page to figure out your final budget for each expense category.

Weekly / Monthly Budget Planning Worksheet

Enter the Final Budget Total from the previous page below:

FINAL BUDGET TOTAL	$

Subtract the Budget Cut Amount for each expense category on page 12 from the Projected Expenses for each expense category on page 10, in order to get your Final Budget Amount for each expense category below:

EXPENSE CATEGORY	PROJECTED EXPENSE	BUDGET CUT AMOUNT	FINAL BUDGET
Food	+$	− $	= $
Transportation	+$	− $	= $
Entertainment	+$	− $	= $
Clothing	+$	− $	= $
Utilities	+$	− $	= $
Shopping	+$	− $	= $
Miscellaneous	+$	− $	= $
Unexpected	+$	− $	= $
Your Own Category #1	+$	− $	= $
Your Own Category #2	+$	− $	= $

Enter these Final Budget Amounts for each of the expense categories on each of the expense category Cost Tracking Worksheets on the subsequent pages.

(Read the important note on the next page.)

Important Note

*If you do not know where to start cutting your budget in each of the expense categories, in order to meet your final budget at the end of the week/month, you may refer to the separate book entitled, **Save Money Checklist Worksheet – Volume 1 & 2** for imaginative and helpful ideas on how to cut expenses, and prevent waste of unnecessary costs in areas you often overlook. It is designed in checklist form for each expense category, and includes worksheets and calculation sheets to manage and track your savings.*

Now, track your costs by each expense category in the following worksheets throughout the week/month; and at the end of the week/month, fill in the Balance Calculation Worksheet on page 65 at the end of this workbook to see if you have met your budget. Manage your expenses everyday throughout the week/month to keep your costs under the budget. (For example, by the half-way point into your week/month, you should not have exceeded 50% of your entire budget for that expense category.)

Cost Tracking Worksheet #1: Food Expenses

Enter the Food Expenses Budget from page 13 below:

Food Expenses Budget	$

RECEIPT #	DATE	DESCRIPTION	AMOUNT	TOTAL	BALANCE
1-3847	9/28	Grocery – Market (Example)	$10·00	$10·00	$690·00
2-528943	9/28	Lunch – Pizza (Example)	$ 5·00	$15·00	$685·00
3-623	9/29	Drink – Pub (Example)	$ 1·50	$16·50	$683·50
4-A709EKJ	10/1	Grocery – Deli (Example)	$12·00	$28·50	$671·50
5-No Receipt	10/2	Leg-of-Lamb for			
		Fishing Bait (Example)	$ 4·00	$32·50	$667·50

RECEIPT #	DATE	DESCRIPTION	AMOUNT	TOTAL	BALANCE

RECEIPT #	DATE	DESCRIPTION	AMOUNT	TOTAL	BALANCE

RECEIPT #	DATE	DESCRIPTION	AMOUNT	TOTAL	BALANCE

RECEIPT #	DATE	DESCRIPTION	AMOUNT	TOTAL	BALANCE

FOOD EXPENSES SUBTOTAL	$

Cost Tracking Worksheet #2: Transportation Expenses

Enter the Transportation Expenses Budget from page 13 below:

Transportation Expenses Budget	$

RECEIPT #	DATE	DESCRIPTION	AMOUNT	TOTAL	BALANCE
1-68387	9/27	Gasoline – A Sta· (Example)	$ 7·00	$ 7·00	$193·00
2-NK520	9/30	Gasoline – B Sta· (Example)	$ 8·00	$15·00	$185·00
3-830615	10/5	Car Insurance (Example)	$15·00	$30·00	$170·00
4-990	10/6	Subway (Example)	$ 2·50	$32·50	$167·50
5-No Receipt	10/9	Personal Private Helicopter			
		Maintenance (Example)	$ 15·00	$47·50	$152·50

RECEIPT #	DATE	DESCRIPTION	AMOUNT	TOTAL	BALANCE

RECEIPT #	DATE	DESCRIPTION	AMOUNT	TOTAL	BALANCE

RECEIPT #	DATE	DESCRIPTION	AMOUNT	TOTAL	BALANCE

RECEIPT #	DATE	DESCRIPTION	AMOUNT	TOTAL	BALANCE

TRANSPORTATION EXPENSES SUBTOTAL	$

Cost Tracking Worksheet #3: Entertainment Expenses

Enter the Entertainment Expenses Budget from page 13 below:

Entertainment Expenses Budget	$

RECEIPT #	DATE	DESCRIPTION	AMOUNT	TOTAL	BALANCE
1-KLZ98	9/25	Movie – A Cine· (Example)	$ 3·00	$ 3·00	$397·00
2-7714	9/27	Concert – B Band (Example)	$ 4·00	$ 7·00	$393·00
3-000894	9/29	Golf – C C·Club (Example)	$ 9·50	$16·50	$383·50
4-112938654	10/5	Ski Trip – D Res· (Example)	$ 6·00	$22·50	$377·50
5-830248	10/7	Masquerade Party Costume			
		Gorilla Suit (Example)	$10·00	$32·50	$367·50

RECEIPT #	DATE	DESCRIPTION	AMOUNT	TOTAL	BALANCE

RECEIPT #	DATE	DESCRIPTION	AMOUNT	TOTAL	BALANCE

RECEIPT #	DATE	DESCRIPTION	AMOUNT	TOTAL	BALANCE

RECEIPT #	DATE	DESCRIPTION	AMOUNT	TOTAL	BALANCE

ENTERTAINMENT EXPENSES SUBTOTAL	$

Cost Tracking Worksheet #4: Clothing Expenses

Enter the Clothing Expenses Budget from page 13 below:

Clothing Expenses Budget	$

RECEIPT #	DATE	DESCRIPTION	AMOUNT	TOTAL	BALANCE
1-53729394	9/26	Sunglasses (Example)	$ 4.00	$ 4.00	$596.00
2-88342	10/1	Gloves - A Dept. (Example)	$ 2.00	$ 6.00	$594.00
3-0298492	10/1	Watch - B Store (Example)	$18.00	$24.00	$576.00
4-JJ18304	10/1	Handbag - C St. (Example)	$ 7.75	$31.75	$568.25
5-574991	10/2	Reversible Two-Tone Color			
		Wig (Example)	$ 5.50	$37.25	$562.75

RECEIPT #	DATE	DESCRIPTION	AMOUNT	TOTAL	BALANCE

RECEIPT #	DATE	DESCRIPTION	AMOUNT	TOTAL	BALANCE

RECEIPT #	DATE	DESCRIPTION	AMOUNT	TOTAL	BALANCE

RECEIPT #	DATE	DESCRIPTION	AMOUNT	TOTAL	BALANCE

CLOTHING EXPENSES SUBTOTAL	$

Cost Tracking Worksheet #5: Utilities Expenses

Enter the Utilities Expenses Budget from page 13 below:

Utilities Expenses Budget	$

RECEIPT #	DATE	DESCRIPTION	AMOUNT	TOTAL	BALANCE
1-8394·2839	9/25	Electricity (Example)	$ 12·00	$12·00	$288·00
2-53843	9/25	Gas (Example)	$ 4·00	$16·00	$284·00
3-231	9/27	Cable TV (Example)	$ 7·00	$23·00	$277·00
4-00389	9/28	Internet (Example)	$ 5·50	$28·50	$271·50
5-77328983	10/2	Electric Eel for Self-			
		Generator (Example)	$ 4·40	$32·90	$267·10

RECEIPT #	DATE	DESCRIPTION	AMOUNT	TOTAL	BALANCE

RECEIPT #	DATE	DESCRIPTION	AMOUNT	TOTAL	BALANCE

RECEIPT #	DATE	DESCRIPTION	AMOUNT	TOTAL	BALANCE

RECEIPT #	DATE	DESCRIPTION	AMOUNT	TOTAL	BALANCE

UTILITIES EXPENSES SUBTOTAL	$

Cost Tracking Worksheet #6: Shopping Expenses

Enter the Shopping Expenses Budget from page 13 below:

Shopping Expenses Budget	$

RECEIPT #	DATE	DESCRIPTION	AMOUNT	TOTAL	BALANCE
1-238	9/27	Dog Food (Example)	$ 2.50	$ 2.50	$897.50
2-91394850	9/28	Pencils – A Store (Example)	$ 1.00	$ 3.50	$896.50
3-7LAGRDN	9/29	Toothpaste (Example)	$ .75	$ 4.25	$895.75
4-S8492	10/2	Piano Lesson (Example)	$15.00	$19.25	$880.75
5-MAX292	10/7	Jack Hammer – B Home			
		Improve S. (Example)	$17.00	$36.25	$863.75

RECEIPT #	DATE	DESCRIPTION	AMOUNT	TOTAL	BALANCE

RECEIPT #	DATE	DESCRIPTION	AMOUNT	TOTAL	BALANCE

RECEIPT #	DATE	DESCRIPTION	AMOUNT	TOTAL	BALANCE

RECEIPT #	DATE	DESCRIPTION	AMOUNT	TOTAL	BALANCE

SHOPPING EXPENSES SUBTOTAL	$

Cost Tracking Worksheet #7: Miscellaneous Expenses

Enter the Miscellaneous Expenses Budget from page 13 below:

Miscellaneous Expenses Budget	$

RECEIPT #	DATE	DESCRIPTION	AMOUNT	TOTAL	BALANCE
1-Check 573	9/25	Mortgage Pay· (Example)	$175·00	$175·00	$825·00
2-Statemt A	9/29	Fitness Club (Example)	$ 10·00	$185·00	$815·00
3-Auto Dep 1	10/1	Tuition – A Sch· (Example)	$ 5·00	$190·00	$810·00
4-Statemt B	10/1	Hospital – Lab· (Example)	$ 14·50	$204·50	$795·50
5-No Receipt	10/3	50 Cattles and			
		1 Piglet (Example)	$200·00	$404·50	$595·50

RECEIPT #	DATE	DESCRIPTION	AMOUNT	TOTAL	BALANCE

RECEIPT #	DATE	DESCRIPTION	AMOUNT	TOTAL	BALANCE

RECEIPT #	DATE	DESCRIPTION	AMOUNT	TOTAL	BALANCE

RECEIPT #	DATE	DESCRIPTION	AMOUNT	TOTAL	BALANCE

MISCELLANEOUS EXPENSES SUBTOTAL	$

Cost Tracking Worksheet #8: Unexpected Expenses

Enter the Unexpected Expenses Budget from page 13 below:

Unexpected Expenses Budget	$

RECEIPT #	DATE	DESCRIPTION	AMOUNT	TOTAL	BALANCE
1-HOSP7981	9/25	Dentist (Example)	$ 7·00	$ 7·00	$493·00
2-8385919	9/27	Flat Tire (Example)	$ 10·00	$ 17·00	$483·00
3-4·2·12AAA	9/27	Express Mail (Example)	$ 5·50	$ 22·50	$477·50
4-XYZ1	10/1	Donation - XYZ (Example)	$ 25·00	$ 47·50	$452·50
5-Statement	10/2-10/7	Childbirth - XYZ General			
		Hospital (Example)	$150·00	$197·50	$302·50

RECEIPT #	DATE	DESCRIPTION	AMOUNT	TOTAL	BALANCE

RECEIPT #	DATE	DESCRIPTION	AMOUNT	TOTAL	BALANCE

RECEIPT #	DATE	DESCRIPTION	AMOUNT	TOTAL	BALANCE

RECEIPT #	DATE	DESCRIPTION	AMOUNT	TOTAL	BALANCE

UNEXPECTED EXPENSES SUBTOTAL	$

Cost Tracking Worksheet #9: Your Own Category #1 Expenses

Enter Your Own Category #1 Expenses Budget from page 13 below:

Your Own Category #1 Expenses Budget	_____	$

RECEIPT #	DATE	DESCRIPTION	AMOUNT	TOTAL	BALANCE

RECEIPT #	DATE	DESCRIPTION	AMOUNT	TOTAL	BALANCE

RECEIPT #	DATE	DESCRIPTION	AMOUNT	TOTAL	BALANCE

RECEIPT #	DATE	DESCRIPTION	AMOUNT	TOTAL	BALANCE

RECEIPT #	DATE	DESCRIPTION	AMOUNT	TOTAL	BALANCE

YOUR OWN CATEGORY #1 EXPENSES SUBTOTAL	$

Cost Tracking Worksheet #10: Your Own Category #2 Expenses

Enter Your Own Category #2 Expenses Budget from page 13 below:

Your Own Category #2 Expenses Budget	_____	$

RECEIPT #	DATE	DESCRIPTION	AMOUNT	TOTAL	BALANCE

RECEIPT #	DATE	DESCRIPTION	AMOUNT	TOTAL	BALANCE

RECEIPT #	DATE	DESCRIPTION	AMOUNT	TOTAL	BALANCE

RECEIPT #	DATE	DESCRIPTION	AMOUNT	TOTAL	BALANCE

RECEIPT #	DATE	DESCRIPTION	AMOUNT	TOTAL	BALANCE

YOUR OWN CATEGORY #2 EXPENSES SUBTOTAL	$

Balance Calculation Worksheet

Enter the Final Budget Total from the Weekly/Monthly Budget Planning Worksheet on page 13 below:

FINAL BUDGET TOTAL	$

Enter the Expenses Subtotals from each of the expense category's Cost Tracking Worksheets on the previous pages below:

EXPENSE CATEGORY	SUBTOTAL
Worksheet #1: Food	$
Worksheet #2: Transportation	$
Worksheet #3: Entertainment	$
Worksheet #4: Clothing	$
Worksheet #5: Utilities	$
Worksheet #6: Shopping	$
Worksheet #7: Miscellaneous	$
Worksheet #8: Unexpected	$
Worksheet #9: Your Own Category #1 _____	$
Worksheet #10: Your Own Category #2 _____	$

Add the Expenses Subtotals on the right column and enter the Expenses Total below:

EXPENSES TOTAL	$

Subtract the Expenses Total from the Final Budget Total to arrive at your Balance Total:

BALANCE TOTAL	$

If your Balance Total is a positive number, you have met your Budget for the week/month. If your Balance Total is a negative number, you have exceeded your budget for the week/month, and you will need to go back to each expense category Cost Tracking Worksheet to find out where you should cut additional expenses next week/month. Use the separate book entitled, "Save Money Checklist Worksheet – Volume 1 & 2" to further manage your cost cutting strategies.

Words Of Advice

Congratulations! You have successfully managed your budget by tracking and controlling your expenses. The first step to planning your finances properly is being aware of the budget that you are working with, and to try to stay within that budget by carefully managing your expenses.

It is impossible to do this without actually laying out each type of expense on paper, and managing those costs on a regular basis to prevent going over the allotted budget. Therefore, it is important that you keep the receipt for each expense, record them, and track your costs carefully to stay within the budget.

It is often difficult to find extra income, so the only way to increase your money is by cutting back costs. You can get the separate book entitled, *Save Money Checklist Worksheet – Volume 1 & 2* by the same author, which will give you helpful ideas on how to save money by cutting back on wasteful expenses that we fail to realize, with calculation worksheets to help you save money. You will be amazed at how much you can save by using a little imagination, and being aware of the wasteful spending that we regularly overlook.

Good luck on your path to becoming a successful financial planner, and saving money to give you that extra pocket change every week/month that you always wanted!

Other Resources Available

Save Money Checklist Worksheet – Volume 1

by Dr. Arthur H. Kebo

at

https://www.createspace.com/3865992

Save Money Checklist Worksheet – Volume 2

by Dr. Arthur H. Kebo

at

https://www.createspace.com/3865993